ABDUL RAHMAN

Blogging Secrets : How to Promote Your Blog Using Skyscraper Technique

Copyright © Abdul Rahman, 2018

All rights reserved. No part of this publication may be reproduced, stored or transmitted in any form or by any means, electronic, mechanical, photocopying, recording, scanning, or otherwise without written permission from the publisher. It is illegal to copy this book, post it to a website, or distribute it by any other means without permission.

First edition

This book was professionally typeset on Reedsy. Find out more at reedsy.com

"I dedicate this piece to All the Bloggers Specially the Newbies in Blogosphere "

By Abdul Rahman

1

What is Blogging?

Blogging is the passion for many since Blogging works on content creation for massive traffic. Several people start various blogs for various purposes such as to inform, to entertain and to influence the readers. There are several Blogging Gurus and content Marketing Specialist having tons of Ideas regarding the Skyscraper approach. Some are of the view that if you pursue the track of Skyscraping you must know that you may fall from it if you implemented the content marketing strategy in wrong way. Remember, the Skyscraper technique does not work for all. Few Bloggers even said that you need to focus on the quality and engaging content and pursue a great marketing plan for it, you may see positive results. So, every content marketer and Blogging guru come forward with an own narrative of skyscraping. Let's find out how we can promote the blog using skyscraper technique. If we research the technique, we will find out that Skyscraper technique works on the following steps:

Blogging has been fun for many but it may require a lot of work out before you reach the heights of success.

The Blogging gurus will be quite aware that the skyscraper

technique is actually a fairly simple method which will enable you to watch the "top content" for any given keyword or any important topic.

2

Keywords and Posts Review

Keywords play a vital role in skyscraper technique as your blog Post must have relevant keywords with high search engine rankings to drive the organic traffic to blog and improving its Google page rank and Alexa ranks. You may find the high-rank keywords with Google and other SEO based sites such Moz, Hubspot or buzz sumo etc as these are the Industry leaders for keyword research.Keyword research also gives the bloggers the idea to choose only high performing keywords.

Review the Top ten ranking Posts on Google :

After Selection of the Keywords, the Next step is to search the Google for above keywords and review the content and marketing technique used by the Bloggers to engage more readers and drive the massive traffic to their sites for the given Keyword. This will give you ideas to craft your blog articles similar to the content you discovered on Google through particular keywords.

Reviewing top ranked posts on search engines like google give you clear idea that Which Headlines and keywords are very important and drive more traffic to your Blog site.

3

Cotent on BuzzSumo

Buzzsumo is the great site to check and analyze top blog posts and it will display the most shared blog posts from these blogs through the selected Keywords you chose and searched the on the tent from the Google.

Buzzsumo is a powerful tool to discover the most shared content from the blogs and enable you to pursue the Skyscraper technique in the true sense. Buzzsumo will also give you key analytics about the low shared Content and the mostly shared content .

The constant use of BuzzSumo will update you about the content performance and the social media network where the content is shared the most and the social media networks where your content is less shared so that you may embed or use Popular search plugins for Social media Marketing purpose .

4

Determine Average length of Top Posts

It is necessary to determine that the average length of top performing content on Google Search engine and craft your own blog post of the same length so that you may get massive organic traffic and drive great traffic to your Blog and improve its ranking.

Several bloggers have implemented this technique and have been extremely Successful in attracting traffic and making a place in Google's top search results.

There are reports that if your publish an over length post or keyword density is intense then there are chances that the search engines may not index the content properly resulting low traffic.

The Posts must be original and must contain an engaging content so that the reader may not get bored in reading the content from the start to finish. The length should be compared with those top blog posts who have higher rank in search engine results .

This detailed analysis will give you the idea that the content you have written after doing some web research and selecting the top keywords is getting hits and views as expected and in return generating a great volume of revenue incase adsense or other advertisements.

5

Identifying Gaps in Competitive Content

Finding gaps in the Top content you search for chosen keywords is very important since it will help you to craft your own blog post by filling gaps and making it more reader and search engine friendly to be liked and shared with first sight.

Gaps will also enable you to improve your blog post and adopt the content marketing approach in your blog posts. Many bloggers do not make the outline properly and leave content gaps which may affect the content marketing strategy.

It is recommended that You must analyze the top content and try to find out the gaps so that you may not repeat the same . If you have identified gaps ,then try to fill the gaps in your content creation strategy .

6

Common Keywords and Phrases used in Competitive Content

Next step is to identify the most relevant keywords and phrases used in the competitive content and consider to use for your blog post son that you may get some traffic through the keywords.

Keywords tags from the top content or competitive content will also improve the blog visibility and authority if checked with Moz domain authority checker. Identifying the Common keywords and phrases and the style of starting the blog post and concluding it will enable you to use the most traffic keywords to drive traffic and promoting your blog content .

The Relevant Keywords and phrases will help discover your content on internet and it will also create backlinks to your blog as people are referred to your blog through clicks . The keywords are imperative to make your content discoverable and keywords relevance will play pivotal role for content exploration and discovery .

7

Writing the Content Outline

Writing the content outline for the top blog is very vital for the logical framework or logical structure from instruction, body and the conclusion.

In the introduction, you will introduce the topic where as in body you will have to distribute the topic in many paragraph or sections, and finally, in conclusion, you will have to sum the ideas or discussion in the Blog post.

The Outline always helps you to discuss the various aspects or parts of the Topic in detail. It is advisable that you must research the topic outline to find engaging headings and subheadings for the content to drive traffic to your blog as Content Marketers always ask a question from the bloggers that if the Visitor Searching for related content finds 10 plus links for any searched terms than they will obviously click the top result first then 2nd and so on .

then why should they visit your link if he finds the answer on first link –simply because you must have more engaging

WRITING THE CONTENT OUTLINE

content and having no content gaps or missing content .

8

Writing 20 to 30 headlines using the Headline Analyzer

The Headline is the magic to attract visitors to the website. The more catchy and creative headline will result in more hits to your blog post. It is necessary that you must write 20 to 30 headlines to find and compare with headline analyzer from Co Schedule.

It will analyze the headlines and display the suggestions and usefulness of the headlines. It will also give you tips to improve the headlines. Therefore, before jumping to write the post you need to analyze the Headline so that it may drive massive traffic to your blog and your blog gains more organic traffic.

9

Create Content for Your Blog Post

Now, after searching a great Headline is the time to write content keeping in view the content length of the top content you searched on the Google.

The content length limitation is necessary because your reader may get bored with too much content and may bounce to other similar site content.

It is also necessary that the content tone should be very informative or How to based step by step as How to or informative content has longer lifeline than raw or boring content. Make your content marketable, readable, informative and engaging to drive the ton of traffic to your Blog.

Therefore, while writing a great blog post, you need to take strict care of the audience, information in hand and presenting the information in logical order.

10

Create Attractive Video that matches the Content

Images present the facts as great informative tools as infographics, images, and Videos add great value to your blog posts. The images should be taken from the web as they will steal your traffic.

It is advisable that you should either create your own infographics or images or get them designed from any design as clear and effective Images and high-definition videos result in more traffic and attract the visitors to your blog.

But if your images are not clear, creative or copied from the web, you have little chances to divert the web traffic and organic traffic towards your Blog.

11

Publishing the Content & Marketing

Congratulations, now you have reached the last button the big one that is published and gives the relief to the bloggers that their Blog posts are going to enter the competitive Content market and compete for its value and space but wait... Before publishing the content, you must proofread the content for any type or grammar errors or broken links.

It is better to use Grammarly app for checking the content and making sure that it is error-free. When you check the all the links you have used in the Blog content are working and there are no any typo or Grammar errors then Go for the Publish Button.Click it and hurray! You have done the most exhausting work.

Promoting Content on Social Media and Content Delivery Networks

The Content which is recently published become the web property of search engines and the search engines will start indexing the fresh content match keywords queries made by the people around the globe.

The search engines display the most searched or top searched content higher as it is shared by the people frequently.

Therefore, it is necessary that you must share the new blog post on social media networks such as Facebook, Twitter, Linkedin, Pinterest, Digg, Stumbleupon and Tumblr etc for driving Social Media traffic to your blog and maximizing content distribution and discovery. If you want to promote through native content Delivery Networks then you may try content.ad, taboo, revcontent, outbrain, Triplelift and blade.

These Native content Ad Networks will distribute across their publisher base and send the tons of traffic to your blog through the content you just published on your blog.

12

Review Performance

Well, we are coming close to this skyscraper Techniques' last Step that is just wait and see the performance of your content and observe tons of traffic coming to your blog.

If you have any monetization plan for your blog, then you may have massive CPM and CPC based earnings if you followed the guidelines strictly and implemented the tools in the true sense.

For performance, you may hook to buzz sumo ,Google Analytics, Alexa Traffic Rankings, Similar web or Moz etc or other popular SEO technique to find out whether the content you just created to compete your competitive content links you had searched and created engaging content for the blog and shared it on social Media as well .

Finally , we reached the point that the Skyscraper content marketing technique is always trending within the marketing industry gurus which was very rare before as trendsetters in blogosphere have reaped tremendous results from this amazing technique but every technique does not work for everybody due to many reasons that do not mean that the Skyscraper Technique is ineffective that is completely wrong.

Maybe, you did not implement the technique in the proper way or maybe you created a content in a nonprofessional may or your headlines and the keywords did not work well or other several reasons.

But the Biggest Bloggers and brands are of the view that this technique gets them big and amazing results.

Moreover, The bloggers also build backlinks which are often called as cash links by the SEO Experts.

As the backlinks are the best way to improve search engine performance of your blog and improve its rankings globally. You may leave comments on forum posts or blog posts of high ranked blogs and earn banks links.

Even guest posting will give you more backlinks or write for the content sites such EzineArticles etc will create several backlinks to your blog site.

13

Final Word

We have reached the final step that is summing up the discussion and tips and concluding it. We have learned that we can implement the Skyscraper technique and can easily promote the content of your blog to next level and drive extensive traffic resulting higher page rank and blog popularity in search engines.

The Blogs promotion technique will only work if you undertake the promotion policy in the sense. The Blogging is the biggest passion and the Blogging success is the key to become popular blogger and influencer across the blogosphere.

Hurray !! You are on the Top of Search Engine Results ....Congratulations!

www.ingramcontent.com/pod-product-compliance
Lightning Source LLC
Chambersburg PA
CBHW041945240526
45473CB00033B/611